LIFE SKILLS

Hygiene

Written by
Steffi Cavell-Clarke

I0895105

KidHaven PUBLISHING

Published in 2027 by
KidHaven Publishing, an Imprint of Greenhaven Publishing, LLC
2544 Clinton St., Buffalo, NY 14224

Written by: Steffi Cavell-Clarke
Edited by: Beth Latham
Designed by: Rob Delph

All facts, statistics, web addresses, and URLs in this book were verified as valid and accurate at time of writing. No responsibility for any changes to external websites or references can be accepted by either the author or publisher.

Cataloging-in-Publication Data

Names: Cavell-Clarke, Steffi.
Title: Hygiene / Steffi Cavell-Clarke.
Description: Buffalo, NY : KidHaven Publishing, 2027. | Series: Life skills | Includes glossary and index.
Identifiers: ISBN 9781534570528 (pbk.) | ISBN 9781534570535 (library bound) | ISBN 9781534570542 (ebook)
Subjects: LCSH: Hygiene--Juvenile literature. | Health behavior--Juvenile literature.
Classification: LCC QP37.C349 2027 | DDC 613.4--dc23

Printed in China

CPSIA compliance information: Batch #QS27KH: For further information contact Greenhaven Publishing LLC at 1-844-317-7404.

Please visit our website, www.greenhavenpublishing.com.
For a free color catalog of all our high-quality books, call toll free 1-844-317-7404 or fax 1-844-317-7405.

Find us on

Image Credits

Images courtesy of Shutterstock.com, unless otherwise stated.
Cover and recurring – Alena Nv, alyona_art86. 2–3 – Odua Images. 4–5 – PeopleImages, HTWE. 6–7 – PeopleImages, il21. 8–9 – Dorde Krstic, Pixel-Shot, matthew25, Bigc Studio, alyona_art86. 10–11 – Paranyu, alyona_art86. 12–13 – New Africa, Alie04. 14–15 – wavebreakmedia, Foxy Fox, ivector, Nsit. 16–17 – wing-wing, Pixel-Shot, GoodStudio. 18–19 – Kmikhidov, Halfpoint. 20–21 – YAKOBCHUK VIACHESLAV, Somkid Saowaros, Pixel-Shot, 5D Media. 22–23 – Melle V, LightField Studios. 24 – GoodStudio, Nsi.

Contents

Words that look like this can be found in the glossary on page 24.

What Are Life Skills?

Life skills are things you learn as you grow up. They help you take care of yourself. Life skills involve doing everyday tasks such as getting dressed, brushing your teeth, saying kind words, and picking up your toys.

Taking care of your body is part of growing up. It helps you stay strong, healthy, and full of energy. Keeping yourself clean is a great way to start.

What Is Hygiene?

Having good hygiene means being clean. Personal hygiene is all about keeping your own body feeling clean and healthy. Your body is amazing, so it is important that you treat it with kindness and respect.

Good hygiene makes it harder for you to get sick. You can practice good hygiene with different parts of your body. Taking care of your skin, nails, hair, and teeth can help you feel your best.

Washing Your Hands

Germs are tiny living things that are too small to see. Some tiny living things are good for us, but germs can make us feel sick. We can protect ourselves from germs by washing our hands often.

WASHING YOUR HANDS IS A SUPER SIMPLE WAY OF KEEPING EVERYONE SAFE, CLEAN, AND HEALTHY.

Washing your hands after using the toilet, after playing outside, and before eating will help get rid of germs and stop them from spreading to other people.

Here is how to wash your hands to make sure that they are super clean.

1

Wet your hands with clean water.

2

Add some soap.

3

Rub your hands together.

4

Rub each palm.

5

Rub all your knuckles.

Rub the inside and back of your fingers.

Rub your thumbs.

Scrub your nails.

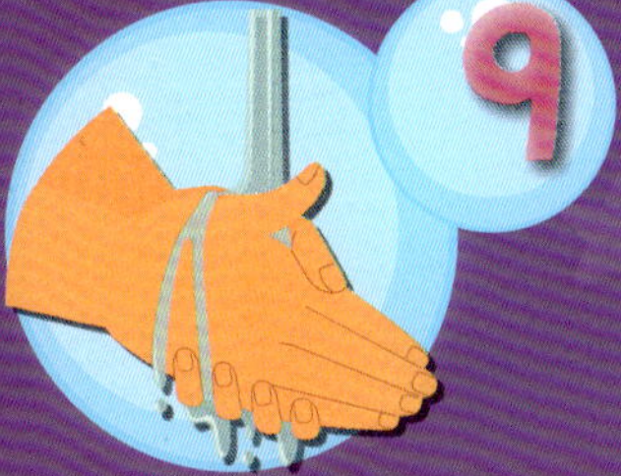

Rinse your hands with clean water.

Dry your hands.

SINGING A SONG SUCH AS THE ALPHABET SONG FOR 20 SECONDS HELPS YOU KNOW HOW LONG TO WASH FOR.

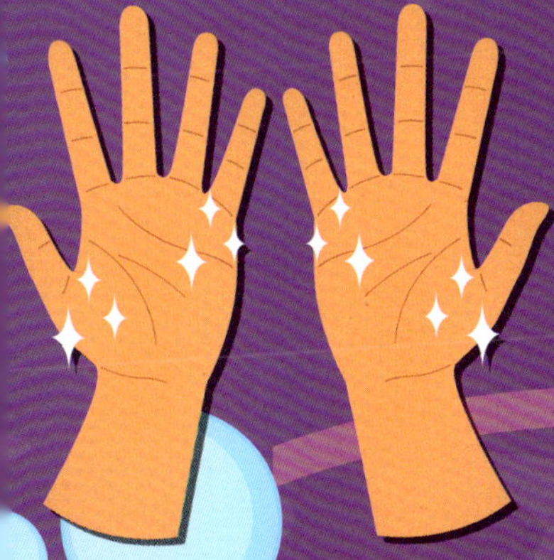

Washing Your Hair and Body

Just like washing your hands, washing your body with soap and water washes away dirt, sweat, and germs. Taking a bath or shower is a good way to wash your body.

YOU CAN ALSO WASH WITH WATER IN THE SINK.

Washing your hair removes dirt and sweat. It leaves you feeling clean.

1. Wet your hair all over.
2. Rub shampoo into your scalp and hair.
3. Rinse it all out with clean water.

Do not get any shampoo in your eyes. It might sting!

Brushing Your Teeth

It is very important to keep your teeth healthy and strong. Bits of food and plaque can cause bad breath and cavities. Brushing twice a day and visiting the dentist will help keep your smile clean and healthy!

All you need is a toothbrush, toothpaste, and clean water.

1 Wet your toothbrush.

2 Add a pea-sized amount of toothpaste.

3 Brush your teeth for two minutes.

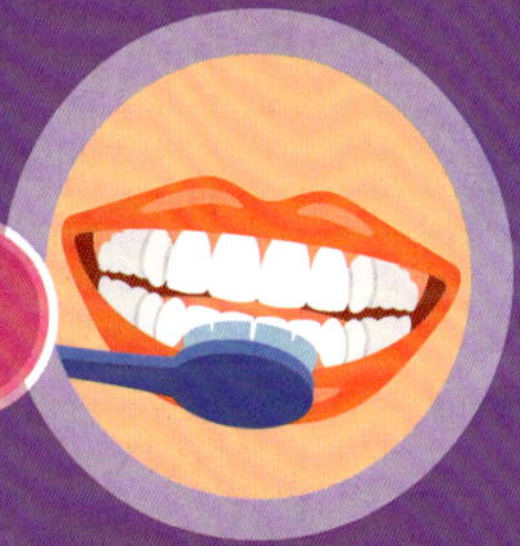

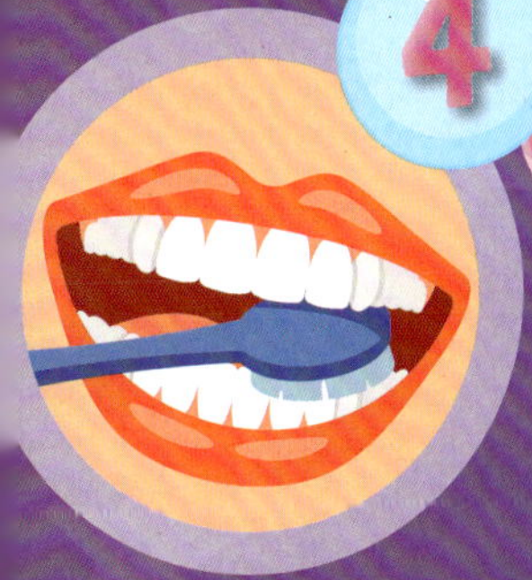

4 Brush every single tooth—front, back, up, and down.

5 Spit into the sink.

6 Rinse your toothbrush to keep it clean.

Wearing Clean Clothes

It is not just our bodies and teeth that get dirty–our clothes do too! When you wear the same clothes for too long, they can get dirty with sweat, food, and germs.

Dirty clothes can make you itchy and smelly.

ASK AN ADULT YOU TRUST IF YOU NEED HELP CHOOSING CLEAN CLOTHES.

Dirty clothes need to go through the <u>laundry</u> to make them clean again. Clean clothes protect your skin and help you feel your best. It is important to wear clean underwear every day too.

Clean Environments

A clean **environment** helps keep us healthy, safe, and happy. When places such as our home and school are clean, there are fewer germs around that might make us feel sick.

Do you like to keep your bedroom clean and neat?

WHEN EVERYONE HELPS, WE CAN MAKE PLACES NICER AND MORE FUN TO LIVE IN.

There are many ways to keep our spaces clean. Keep food areas clean by throwing out garbage and old food. Clean up after yourself by flushing and washing your hands after using the toilet.

Coughs and Sneezes

We all get sick sometimes. It is part of life. Colds and coughs are very common. They spread through tiny germs that enter your body. Having good hygiene can help spread fewer germs.

When you need to cough, cough into your elbow. When you need to sneeze, sneeze into a tissue and throw it into the trash. This will help to spread fewer germs and keep you and your friends healthy.

Remember to:

1 CATCH IT

with a tissue

2 THROW IT

throw the tissue in the trash

3 CLEAN IT

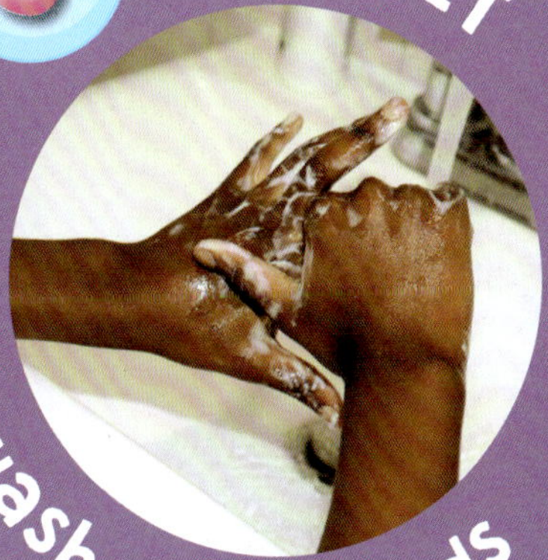

wash your hands

Getting Dirty!

Everybody gets dirty sometimes! It is impossible to be clean all the time. Playing outside, exploring, creating new things, and having fun can often make you a little dirty. That is normal!

Dirt washes off, but the fun and memories last forever!

Washing away the dirt, sweat, and germs keeps you smelling good and feeling comfortable. It helps you stay healthy. It is important to start and end the day with a clean body to keep you feeling your best.

Scrub-a-dub-dub!

Glossary

CAVITIES holes made in teeth

ENERGY the power that makes living things able to move and live

ENVIRONMENT the surroundings that an animal, plant, or human lives in

LAUNDRY the process of washing and cleaning clothes

PLAQUE the sticky layer made on teeth by germs

RESPECT feeling that something or someone is important

SCALP skin on top of your head

SWEAT tiny liquid droplets made by the body when it is too hot

Index